family favorites
muffins &
cupcakes

Bath · New York · Singapore · Hong Kong · Cologne · Delhi · Melbourne

apple & cinnamon muffins

ingredients

MAKES 6

3 oz/85 g/scant $^2/_3$ cup all-
  purpose whole-wheat flour
$2^1/_2$ oz/70 g/$^1/_2$ cup all-
  purpose white flour
$1^1/_2$ tsp baking powder
pinch of salt
1 tsp ground cinnamon
$1^1/_2$ oz/40 g/scant $^1/_4$ cup
  golden superfine sugar
2 small eating apples, peeled,
  cored, and finely chopped
4 fl oz/125 ml/$^1/_2$ cup milk
1 egg, beaten
4 tbsp butter, melted

topping

12 brown sugar lumps,
  coarsely crushed
$^1/_2$ tsp ground cinnamon

method

1 Place 6 muffin paper liners in a muffin pan.

2 Sift both flours, baking powder, salt, and cinnamon together into a large bowl and stir in the sugar and chopped apples. Place the milk, egg, and butter in a separate bowl and mix. Add the wet ingredients to the dry ingredients and gently stir until just combined.

3 Divide the batter evenly among the paper liners. To make the topping, mix the crushed sugar lumps and cinnamon together and sprinkle over the muffins. Bake in a preheated oven, 400°F/ 200°C, for 20–25 minutes, or until risen and golden. Remove the muffins from the oven and serve warm or place them on a cooling rack and let cool.

banana pecan muffins

ingredients

MAKES 8

$5^{1}/_{2}$ oz/150 g/generous 1 cup
   all-purpose flour

$1^{1}/_{2}$ tsp baking powder

pinch of salt

$2^{1}/_{2}$ oz/70 g/$^{1}/_{3}$ cup golden
   superfine sugar

4 oz/115 g/1 cup shelled
   pecans, coarsely chopped

2 large ripe bananas, mashed

5 tbsp milk

2 tbsp butter, melted

1 large egg, beaten

$^{1}/_{2}$ tsp vanilla extract

method

1 Place 8 muffin paper liners in a muffin pan. Sift the flour, baking powder, and salt into a bowl, add the sugar and pecans, and stir to combine.

2 Place the mashed bananas, milk, butter, egg, and vanilla extract in a separate bowl and mix together. Add the wet ingredients to the dry ingredients and gently stir until just combined.

3 Divide the batter evenly among the paper liners and bake in a preheated oven, 375°F/ 190°C, for 20–25 minutes until risen and golden. Remove the muffins from the oven and place them on a cooling rack and let cool.

blueberry muffins

ingredients

MAKES 12

vegetable oil cooking spray,
   for oiling (if using)

8 oz/225 g/generous
   1^1/$_2$ cups all-purpose flour

1 tsp baking soda

^{1}/$_4$ tsp salt

1 tsp allspice

4 oz/115 g/generous ^{1}/$_2$ cup
   superfine sugar

3 large egg whites

3 tbsp lowfat margarine

5 fl oz/150 ml/^{2}/$_3$ cup
   thick lowfat plain or
   blueberry-flavored yogurt

1 tsp vanilla extract

3 oz/85 g/^{3}/$_4$ cup
   fresh blueberries

method

1 Spray a 12-cup muffin pan with vegetable oil cooking spray, or line it with 12 muffin paper liners.

2 Sift the flour, baking soda, salt, and half of the allspice into a large mixing bowl. Add 6 tablespoons of the superfine sugar and mix together.

3 In a separate bowl, whisk the egg whites together. Add the margarine, yogurt, and vanilla extract and mix together well, then stir in the fresh blueberries until thoroughly mixed. Add the fruit mixture to the flour mixture, then gently stir together until just combined. Do not overstir the batter—it is fine for it to be a little lumpy.

4 Divide the muffin batter evenly among the 12 cups in the muffin pan or the paper liners (they should be about two-thirds full). Mix the remaining sugar with the remaining allspice, then sprinkle the mixture over the muffins. Transfer to a preheated oven, 375°F/190°C, and bake for 25 minutes, or until risen and golden. Remove the muffins from the oven and serve warm, or place them on a cooling rack and let cool.

spiced chocolate muffins

ingredients

MAKES 12

$3^1/2$ oz/100 g butter, softened

5 oz/150 g/scant $^3/4$ cup
   superfine sugar

4 oz/115 g/$^1/2$ cup packed
   brown sugar

2 large eggs

5 fl oz/150 ml/$^2/3$ cup
   sour cream

5 tbsp milk

9 oz/250 g/generous
   $1^3/4$ cups all-purpose flour

1 tsp baking soda

2 tbsp unsweetened cocoa

1 tsp allspice

7 oz/200 g/generous 1 cup
   semisweet chocolate chips

method

1 Line a 12-cup muffin pan with muffin liners.

2 Place the butter, superfine sugar, and brown sugar in a bowl and beat well. Beat in the eggs, sour cream, and milk until thoroughly mixed. Sift the flour, baking soda, cocoa, and allspice into a separate bowl and stir into the mixture. Add the chocolate chips and mix well. Divide the batter evenly among the paper liners. Bake in a preheated oven, 375°F/190°C, for 25–30 minutes.

3 Remove from the oven and let cool for 10 minutes. Place them on a cooling rack and let cool completely. Store in an airtight container until required.

double chocolate muffins

ingredients

MAKES 12

7 oz/200 g/scant $1^1/_2$ cups
    all-purpose flour
1 oz/25 g/$^1/_3$ cup
    unsweetened cocoa, plus
    extra for dusting
1 tbsp baking powder
1 tsp ground cinnamon
4 oz/115 g/generous $^1/_2$ cup
    golden superfine sugar
$6^1/_2$ oz/185 g white chocolate,
    broken into pieces
2 large eggs
$3^1/_2$ fl oz/100 ml/generous
    $^1/_3$ cup sunflower
    or peanut oil
7 fl oz/200 ml/1 cup milk

method

1 Line a 12-cup muffin pan with muffin liners.

2 Sift the flour, cocoa, baking powder, and cinnamon into a large mixing bowl. Stir in the sugar and $4^1/_2$ oz/125 g of the white chocolate.

3 Place the eggs and oil in a separate bowl and whisk until frothy, then gradually whisk in the milk. Stir into the dry ingredients until just blended. Divide the batter evenly among the paper liners, filling each three-quarters full. Bake in a preheated oven, 400°F/200°C, for 20 minutes, or until well risen and springy to the touch. Remove the muffins from the oven, let cool in the pan for 2 minutes, then remove them and place them on a cooling rack to cool completely.

4 Place the remaining white chocolate in a heatproof bowl, set the bowl over a pan of barely simmering water, and heat until melted. Spread over the top of the muffins. Let set, then dust the tops with a little cocoa and serve.

chocolate chip muffins

ingredients

MAKES 12

3 tbsp soft margarine

7 oz/200 g/1 cup
  superfine sugar

2 large eggs

5 fl oz/150 ml/^{2}/$_3$ cup
  whole plain yogurt

5 tbsp milk

10 oz/300 g/2 cups
  all-purpose flour

1 tsp baking soda

4 oz/115 g/1 cup semisweet
  chocolate chips

method

1 Line a 12-cup muffin pan with muffin liners.

2 Place the margarine and sugar in a mixing bowl and beat with a wooden spoon until light and fluffy. Beat in the eggs, yogurt, and milk until combined.

3 Sift the flour and baking soda into the batter. Stir until just blended.

4 Stir in the chocolate chips, then divide the batter evenly among the paper liners and bake in a preheated oven, 400°F/200°C, for 25 minutes, or until risen and golden. Remove the muffins from the oven and let cool in the pan for 5 minutes, then place them on a cooling rack to cool completely.

doughnut muffins

ingredients

MAKES 12

6 oz/175 g butter, softened,
    plus extra for greasing

7 oz/200 g/1 cup
    superfine sugar

2 large eggs, lightly beaten

13oz/375g/generous
    2^1/$_2$ cups all-purpose flour

^{3}/$_4$ tbsp baking powder

^{1}/$_4$ tsp baking soda

pinch of salt

^{1}/$_2$ tsp freshly grated nutmeg

9 fl oz/250 ml/generous
    1 cup milk

topping

3^1/$_2$ oz/100 g/^{1}/$_2$ cup
    superfine sugar

1 tsp ground cinnamon

2 tbsp butter, melted

method

1 Grease a deep 12-cup muffin pan. In a large bowl, beat the butter and sugar together until light and creamy. Add the eggs, a little at a time, beating well between additions.

2 Sift the flour, baking powder, baking soda, salt, and nutmeg together. Add half to the creamed mixture with half of the milk. Gently fold the ingredients together before incorporating the remaining flour and milk. Spoon the mixture into the prepared muffin pan, filling each hole to about two-thirds full. Bake in a preheated oven, 350°F/180°C, for 15–20 minutes, or until the muffins are lightly brown and firm to the touch.

3 For the topping, mix the sugar and cinnamon together. While the muffins are still warm from the oven, brush lightly with melted butter, and sprinkle over the cinnamon and sugar mixture. Eat warm or cold.

apple streusel cupcakes

ingredients

MAKES 14

$^1/_2$ tsp baking soda

10-oz/280-g jar tart applesauce

4 tbsp butter, softened,
　　or soft margarine

3 oz/85 g/scant $^1/_2$ cup raw
　　brown sugar

1 large egg, lightly beaten

6 oz/175 g/scant $1^1/_4$ cups
　　self-rising white flour

$^1/_2$ tsp ground cinnamon

$^1/_2$ tsp freshly ground nutmeg

topping

$1^3/_4$ oz/50 g/generous $^1/_3$ cup
　　all-purpose flour

$1^3/_4$ oz/50 g/$^1/_4$ cup
　　raw brown sugar

$^1/_4$ tsp ground cinnamon

$^1/_4$ tsp freshly grated nutmeg

$2^1/_2$ tbsp butter

method

1 Put 14 paper baking cases in a muffin pan, or place 14 double-layer paper cases on a cookie sheet.

2 First make the topping. Put the flour, sugar, cinnamon, and nutmeg in a bowl or in the bowl of a food processor. Cut the butter into small pieces, then either rub it in by hand or blend in the processor until the mixture resembles fine bread crumbs. Set aside while you make the cakes.

3 To make the cupcakes, add the baking soda to the jar of applesauce and stir until dissolved. Put the butter and sugar in a bowl and beat together until light and fluffy. Gradually beat in the egg. Sift in the flour, cinnamon, and nutmeg and, using a large metal spoon, fold into the mixture, alternating with the applesauce.

4 Spoon the batter into the paper cases. Sprinkle the topping over each cupcake to cover the tops and press down gently.

5 Bake the cupcakes in a preheated oven, 350°F/180°C, for 20 minutes, or until well risen and golden brown. Leave the cakes for 2–3 minutes before serving warm or transfer to a wire rack and let cool.

carrot & orange cupcakes with mascarpone frosting

ingredients

MAKES 12

8 tbsp butter, softened,
  or soft margarine
4 oz/115 g/generous $^1/_2$ cup
  firmly packed brown sugar
juice and finely grated rind of
  1 small orange
2 large eggs, lightly beaten
6 oz/175 g carrots, grated
1 oz/25 g/$^1/_4$ cup walnut
  pieces, coarsely chopped
4$^1/_2$ oz/125 g/scant 1 cup
  all-purpose flour
1 tsp ground pumpkin pie spice
1$^1/_2$ tsp baking powder

frosting

10 oz/280 g/1$^1/_4$ cups
  mascarpone cheese
4 tbsp confectioners' sugar
grated rind of 1 large orange

method

1 Put 12 muffin paper cases in a muffin pan.

2 Put the butter, sugar, and orange rind in a bowl and beat together until light and fluffy. Gradually add the eggs, beating well after each addition. Squeeze any excess liquid from the carrots and add to the mixture with the walnuts and orange juice. Stir into the mixture until well mixed. Sift in the flour, pumpkin pie spice, and baking powder and then, using a metal spoon, fold into the mixture. Spoon the batter into the paper cases.

3 Bake the cupcakes in a preheated oven, 350°F/180°C, for 25 minutes, or until well risen, firm to the touch, and golden brown. Transfer to a wire rack and let cool.

4 To make the frosting, put the mascarpone cheese, confectioners' sugar, and orange rind in a large bowl and beat together until well mixed.

5 When the cupcakes are cold, spread the frosting on top of each, swirling it with a round-bladed knife. Store the cupcakes in the refrigerator until ready to serve.

warm strawberry cupcakes baked in a teacup

ingredients

MAKES 6

8 tbsp butter, softened,
    plus extra for greasing

4 tbsp strawberry conserve

4 oz/115 g/generous ½ cup
    superfine sugar

2 eggs, lightly beaten

1 tsp vanilla extract

4 oz/115 g/generous ¾ cup
    self-rising white flour

1 lb/450 g small whole fresh
    strawberries

confectioners' sugar,
    for dusting

method

1 Grease 6 heavy, round teacups with butter. Spoon 2 teaspoons of the strawberry conserve in the bottom of each teacup.

2 Put the butter and sugar in a bowl and beat together until light and fluffy. Gradually add the eggs, beating well after each addition, then add the vanilla extract. Sift in the flour and, using a large metal spoon, fold it into the mixture. Spoon the batter into the teacups.

3 Stand the cups in a roasting pan, then pour in enough hot water to come one-third up the sides of the cups. Bake the cupcakes in a preheated oven, 350°F/180°C, for 40 minutes, or until well risen and golden brown, and a skewer, inserted in the center, comes out clean. If over-browning, cover the cupcakes with a sheet of foil. Leave the cupcakes to cool for 2–3 minutes, then carefully lift the cups from the pan and place them on saucers.

4 Place a few of the whole strawberries on each cake, then dust them with a little sifted confectioners' sugar. Serve warm with the remaining strawberries.

frosted peanut butter cupcakes

ingredients

MAKES 16

4 tbsp butter, softened,
　　or soft margarine
8 oz/225 g/scant 1^{1}/$_{4}$ cups
　　firmly packed brown sugar
4 oz/115 g/generous ^{1}/$_{3}$ cup
　　crunchy peanut butter
2 eggs, lightly beaten
1 tsp vanilla extract
8 oz/225 g/generous
　　1^{1}/$_{2}$ cups all-purpose flour
2 tsp baking powder
3^{1}/$_{2}$ fl oz/100 ml/generous
　　^{1}/$_{3}$ cup milk

frosting

7 oz/200 g/scant 1 cup
　　full-fat soft cream cheese
2 tbsp butter, softened
8 oz/225 g/2 cups
　　confectioners' sugar

method

1 Put 16 muffin paper cases in a muffin pan.

2 Put the butter, sugar, and peanut butter in a bowl and beat together for 1–2 minutes, or until well mixed. Gradually add the eggs, beating well after each addition, then add the vanilla extract. Sift in the flour and baking powder and then, using a metal spoon, fold them into the mixture, alternating with the milk. Spoon the batter into the paper cases.

3 Bake the cupcakes in a preheated oven, 350°F/180°C, for 25 minutes, or until well risen and golden brown. Transfer to a wire rack and let cool.

4 To make the frosting, put the cream cheese and butter in a large bowl and, using an electric hand whisk, beat together until smooth. Sift the confectioners' sugar into the mixture, then beat together until well mixed.

5 When the cupcakes are cold, spread the frosting on top of each cupcake, swirling it with a round-bladed knife. Store the cupcakes in the refrigerator until ready to serve.

dark & white fudge cupcakes

ingredients

MAKES 20

7 fl oz/100 ml/scant
    1 cup water
6 tbsp butter
3 oz/85 g/scant $^1/_2$ cup
    superfine sugar
1 tbsp corn syrup
3 tbsp milk
1 tsp vanilla extract
1 tsp baking soda
8 oz/225 g/generous
    1$^1/_2$ cups all-purpose flour
2 tbsp unsweetened cocoa

topping

1$^3/_4$ oz/50 g semisweet
    chocolate
4 tbsp water
3$^1/_2$ tbsp butter
1$^3/_4$ oz/50 g white chocolate
12 oz/350 g/3 cups
    confectioners' sugar

chocolate curls

3$^1/_2$ oz/100 g semisweet
    chocolate
3$^1/_2$ oz/100 g white chocolate

method

1 Put 20 paper baking cases in 2 muffin pans, or place 20 double-layer paper cases on 2 baking sheets.

2 Put the water, butter, superfine sugar, and syrup in a pan. Heat gently, stirring, until the sugar has dissolved, then bring to a boil. Reduce the heat and cook gently for 5 minutes. Remove from the heat and let cool.

3 Meanwhile, put the milk and vanilla extract in a bowl. Add the baking soda and stir to dissolve. Sift the flour and cocoa into a separate bowl and add the syrup mixture. Stir in the milk and beat until smooth. Spoon the batter into the paper cases until they are two-thirds full. Bake the cupcakes in a preheated oven, 350°F/180°C, for 20 minutes, or until well risen and firm to the touch. Transfer to a wire rack and let cool.

4 To make the topping, break the semisweet chocolate into a small heatproof bowl, add half the water and half the butter, and melt over a pan of gently simmering water. Stir until smooth and let stand over the water. Using another bowl, repeat with the white chocolate and remaining water and butter. Sift half the sugar into each bowl and beat until smooth and thick. Top the cupcakes with the frostings and let set. Decorate with chocolate curls made by shaving the chocolate with a potato peeler.

warm molten-centered chocolate cupcakes

ingredients

MAKES 8

4 tbsp soft margarine

2 oz/55 g/generous $\frac{1}{4}$ cup
superfine sugar

1 large egg

3 oz/85 g/generous $\frac{1}{2}$ cup
self-rising flour

1 tbsp unsweetened cocoa

2 oz/55 g semisweet
chocolate

confectioners' sugar,
for dusting

method

1 Put 8 paper baking cases in a muffin pan, or place 8 double-layer paper cases on a cookie sheet.

2 Put the margarine, sugar, egg, flour, and cocoa in a large bowl and, using an electric hand whisk, beat together until just smooth.

3 Spoon half of the batter into the paper cases. Using a teaspoon, make an indentation in the center of each cake. Break the chocolate evenly into 8 squares and place a piece in each indentation, then spoon the remaining cake batter on top.

4 Bake the cupcakes in a preheated oven, 375°F/190°C, for 20 minutes, or until well risen and springy to the touch. Leave the cupcakes for 2–3 minutes before serving warm, dusted with sifted confectioners' sugar.

mocha cupcakes with whipped cream

ingredients

MAKES 20

2 tbsp instant espresso
    coffee powder

6 tbsp butter

3 oz/85 g/scant $^1/_2$ cup
    superfine sugar

1 tbsp honey

7 fl oz/200 ml/scant 1 cup
    water

8 oz/225 g/generous
    $1^1/_2$ cups all-purpose flour

2 tbsp unsweetened cocoa

1 tsp baking soda

3 tbsp milk

1 large egg, lightly beaten

topping

8 fl oz/225 ml/1 cup
    whipping cream

unsweetened cocoa, sifted,
    for dusting

method

1 Put 20 paper baking cases in 2 muffin pans, or place 20 double-layer paper cases on 2 baking sheets.

2 Put the coffee powder, butter, sugar, honey, and water in a pan and heat gently, stirring, until the sugar has dissolved. Bring to a boil, then reduce the heat and let simmer for 5 minutes. Pour into a large heatproof bowl and let cool.

3 When the mixture has cooled, sift in the flour and cocoa. Dissolve the baking soda in the milk, then add to the mixture with the egg and beat together until smooth. Spoon the batter into the paper cases.

4 Bake the cupcakes in a preheated oven, 350°F/180°C, for 15–20 minutes, or until well risen and firm to the touch. Transfer to a wire rack to cool.

5 For the topping, whisk the cream in a bowl until it holds its shape. Just before serving, spoon heaped teaspoonfuls of cream on top of each cake, then dust lightly with sifted cocoa. Store the cupcakes in the refrigerator until ready to serve.

tiny chocolate cupcakes with ganache frosting

ingredients

MAKES 20

4 tbsp butter, softened

2 oz/55 g/generous $^1/_4$ cup
   superfine sugar

1 large egg, lightly beaten

2 oz/55 g/scant $^1/_2$ cup white
   self-rising flour

2 tbsp unsweetened cocoa

1 tbsp milk

20 chocolate-coated coffee
   beans, to decorate
   (optional)

frosting

3$^1/_2$ oz/100 g semisweet
   chocolate

3$^1/_2$ fl oz/100 ml/generous
   $^1/_3$ cup heavy cream

method

1 Put 20 double-layer mini paper cases on 2 baking sheets.

2 Put the butter and sugar in a bowl and beat together until light and fluffy. Gradually beat in the egg. Sift in the flour and cocoa and then, using a metal spoon, fold them into the mixture. Stir in the milk.

3 Fill a pastry bag, fitted with a large plain tip, with the batter and pipe it into the paper cases, filling each one until half full.

4 Bake the cakes in a preheated oven, 375°F/ 190°C, for 10–15 minutes, or until well risen and firm to the touch. Transfer to a wire rack to cool.

5 To make the frosting, break the chocolate into a pan and add the cream. Heat gently, stirring all the time, until the chocolate has melted. Pour into a large heatproof bowl and, using an electric hand whisk, beat the mixture for 10 minutes, or until thick, glossy and cool.

6 Fill a pastry bag, fitted with a large star tip, with the frosting and pipe a swirl on top of each cupcake. Alternatively, spoon over the frosting. Chill in the refrigerator for 1 hour before serving. Serve decorated with a chocolate-coated coffee bean, if liked.

devil's food cakes with chocolate frosting

ingredients

MAKES 18

$3^1/_2$ tbsp soft margarine

4 oz/115 g/generous $^1/_2$ cup
 firmly packed brown sugar

2 large eggs

4 oz/115 g/generous $^3/_4$ cup
 all-purpose flour

$^1/_2$ tsp baking soda

1 oz/25 g/generous $^1/_4$ cup
 unsweetened cocoa

4 fl oz/125 ml/$^1/_2$ cup
 sour cream

frosting

$4^1/_2$ oz/125 g semisweet
 chocolate

2 tbsp superfine sugar

5 fl oz/150 ml/$^2/_3$ cup
 sour cream

chocolate curls
 (optional)

$3^1/_2$ oz/100 g semisweet
 chocolate

method

1 Put 18 paper baking cases in a muffin pan, or put 18 double-layer paper cases on a cookie sheet.

2 Put the margarine, sugar, eggs, flour, baking soda, and cocoa in a large bowl and, using an electric hand whisk, beat together until just smooth. Using a metal spoon, fold in the sour cream. Spoon the batter into the paper cases.

3 Bake the cupcakes in a preheated oven, 350°F/180°C, for 20 minutes, or until well risen and firm to the touch. Transfer to a wire rack to cool.

4 To make the frosting, break the chocolate into a heatproof bowl. Set the bowl over a pan of gently simmering water and heat until melted, stirring occasionally. Remove from the heat and let cool slightly, then whisk in the sugar and sour cream until combined. Spread the frosting over the tops of the cupcakes and let set in the refrigerator before serving. If liked, serve decorated with chocolate curls made by shaving semisweet chocolate with a potato peeler.

rose petal cupcakes

ingredients

MAKES 12

8 tbsp butter, softened

4 oz/115 g/generous $1/2$ cup
   superfine sugar

2 eggs, lightly beaten

1 tbsp milk

few drops of extract of rose oil

$1/4$ tsp vanilla extract

6 oz/175 g/scant $1^1/4$ cups
   self-rising white flour

frosting

6 tbsp butter, softened

6 oz/175 g/$1^1/2$ cups
   confectioners' sugar

pink or purple food coloring
   (optional)

silver dragées (cake decoration
   balls), to decorate

candied rose petals

12–24 rose petals

lightly beaten egg white,
   for brushing

superfine sugar, for sprinkling

method

1 To make the candied rose petals, gently rinse the petals and dry well with paper towels. Using a pastry brush, paint both sides of a rose petal with egg white, then coat well with superfine sugar. Place on a tray and repeat with the remaining petals. Cover the tray with foil and let dry overnight.

2 Put 12 paper baking cases in a muffin pan, or place 12 double-layer paper cases on a cookie sheet.

3 Put the butter and sugar in a bowl and beat together until light and fluffy. Gradually add the eggs, beating well after each addition. Stir in the milk, rose oil extract, and vanilla extract then, using a metal spoon, fold in the flour. Spoon the batter into the paper cases.

4 Bake the cupcakes in a preheated oven, 400°F/200°C, for 12–15 minutes until well risen and golden brown. Transfer to a wire rack and let cool.

5 To make the frosting, put the butter in a large bowl and beat until fluffy. Sift in the confectioners' sugar and mix well together. If wished, add a few drops of pink or purple food coloring to complement the rose petals.

6 When the cupcakes are cold, spread the frosting on top of each cake. Top with 1–2 candied rose petals and sprinkle with silver dragées to decorate.

feather-frosted coffee cupcakes

ingredients

MAKES 16

1 tbsp instant coffee granules

1 tbsp boiling water

8 tbsp butter, softened,
    or soft margarine

4 oz/115 g/generous $1/2$ cup
    firmly packed brown sugar

2 eggs

4 oz/115 g/generous $3/4$ cup
    self-rising white flour

$1/2$ tsp baking powder

2 tbsp sour cream

frosting

8 oz/225 g/2 cups
    confectioners' sugar

4 tsp warm water

1 tsp instant coffee granules

2 tsp boiling water

method

1 Put 16 paper baking cases in a muffin pan, or place 16 double-layer paper cases on a cookie sheet.

2 Put the coffee granules in a cup or small bowl, add the boiling water, and stir until dissolved. Let cool slightly.

3 Put the butter, sugar, and eggs in a bowl. Sift in the flour and baking powder, then beat the ingredients together until smooth. Add the dissolved coffee and the sour cream and beat together until well mixed. Spoon the batter into the paper cases. Bake in a preheated oven, 375°F/190°C, for 20 minutes, or until well risen and golden brown. Transfer to a wire rack and let cool.

4 To make the frosting, sift $3/4$ cup of the confectioners' sugar into a bowl, then gradually mix in the warm water to make a coating consistency that will cover the back of a wooden spoon. Dissolve the coffee granules in the boiling water. Sift the remaining confectioners' sugar into a bowl, then stir in the dissolved coffee granules. Spoon the frosting into a pastry bag fitted with a piping tip. When the cupcakes are cold, coat the tops with the white frosting, then quickly pipe the coffee frosting in parallel lines on top. Using a skewer, draw it across the piped lines in both directions. Let set before serving.

lemon butterfly cakes

ingredients

MAKES 12

4 oz/115 g/generous $^3/_4$ cup
    self-rising white flour

$^1/_2$ tsp baking powder

8 tbsp soft margarine

4 oz/115 g/generous $^1/_2$ cup
    superfine sugar

2 eggs, lightly beaten

finely grated rind of $^1/_2$ lemon

2 tbsp milk

confectioners' sugar,
    for dusting

lemon filling

6 tbsp butter, softened

6 oz/175 g/1$^1/_2$ cups
    confectioners' sugar

1 tbsp lemon juice

method

1 Put 12 paper baking cases in a muffin pan, or place 12 double-layer paper cases on a cookie sheet.

2 Sift the flour and baking powder into a large bowl. Add the margarine, sugar, eggs, lemon rind, and milk and, using an electric hand whisk, beat together until smooth. Spoon the batter into the paper cases.

3 Bake the cupcakes in a preheated oven, 375°F/190°C, for 15–20 minutes, or until well risen and golden brown. Transfer to a wire rack and let cool.

4 To make the filling, put the butter in a bowl and beat until fluffy. Sift in the confectioners' sugar, add the lemon juice, and beat together until smooth and creamy.

5 When the cupcakes are cold, use a serrated knife to cut a circle from the top of each cupcake and then cut each circle in half. Spread or pipe a little of the buttercream filling into the center of each cupcake, then press the 2 semicircular halves into it at an angle to resemble butterfly wings. Dust with sifted confectioners' sugar before serving.

sticky gingerbread cupcakes

ingredients

MAKES 16

4 oz/115 g/generous $^3/_4$ cup
   all-purpose flour

2 tsp ground ginger

$^3/_4$ tsp ground cinnamon

1 piece of preserved
   ginger, minced

$^3/_4$ tsp baking soda

4 tbsp milk

6 tbsp butter, softened,
   or soft margarine

$2^1/_2$ oz/70 g/generous $^1/_3$ cup
   firmly packed brown sugar

2 tbsp molasses

2 eggs, lightly beaten

pieces of preserved ginger,
   to decorate

frosting

6 tbsp butter, softened

6 oz/175 g/1$^1/_2$ cups
   confectioners' sugar

2 tbsp ginger syrup from the
   preserved ginger jar

method

1 Put 16 paper baking cases in a muffin pan, or place 16 double-layer paper cases on a cookie sheet.

2 Sift the flour, ground ginger, and cinnamon together into a bowl. Add the minced ginger and toss in the flour mixture until well coated. In a separate bowl, dissolve the baking soda in the milk.

3 Put the butter and sugar in a bowl and beat together until fluffy. Beat in the molasses, then gradually add the eggs, beating well after each addition. Beat in the flour mixture, then gradually beat in the milk. Spoon the batter into the paper cases.

4 Bake the cupcakes in a preheated oven, 325°F/160°C, for 20 minutes, or until well risen and golden brown. Transfer to a wire rack and let cool.

5 To make the frosting, put the butter in a bowl and beat until fluffy. Sift in the sugar, add the ginger syrup, and beat together until smooth and creamy. Slice the preserved ginger into thin slivers or chop finely.

6 When the cupcakes are cold, spread the frosting on top of each cupcake, then decorate with pieces of ginger.

drizzled honey cupcakes

ingredients

MAKES 12

3 oz/85 g/generous $^1/_2$ cup
　　self-rising white flour

$^1/_4$ tsp ground cinnamon

pinch of ground cloves

pinch of grated nutmeg

6 tbsp butter, softened

3 oz/85 g/scant $^1/_2$ cup
　　superfine sugar

1 tbsp honey

finely grated rind of 1 orange

2 eggs, lightly beaten

$1^1/_2$ oz/40 g/$^3/_4$ cup walnut
　　pieces, minced

topping

$^1/_2$ oz/15 g/$^1/_8$ cup walnut
　　pieces, minced

$^1/_4$ tsp ground cinnamon

2 tbsp honey

juice of 1 orange

method

1 Put 12 paper baking cases in a muffin pan, or place 12 double-layer paper cases on a cookie sheet.

2 Sift the flour, cinnamon, cloves, and nutmeg together into a bowl. Put the butter and sugar in a separate bowl and beat together until light and fluffy. Beat in the honey and orange rind, then gradually add the eggs, beating well after each addition. Using a metal spoon, fold in the flour mixture. Stir in the walnuts, then spoon the batter into the paper cases.

3 Bake the cupcakes in a preheated oven, 375°F/190°C, for 20 minutes, or until well risen and golden brown. Transfer to a wire rack and let cool.

4 To make the topping, mix together the walnuts and cinnamon. Put the honey and orange juice in a pan and heat gently, stirring, until combined.

5 When the cupcakes have almost cooled, prick the tops all over with a fork or skewer and then drizzle with the warm honey mixture. Sprinkle the walnut mixture over the top of each cupcake and serve warm or cold.

marbled chocolate cupcakes

ingredients

MAKES 21

6 oz/175 g/^{3}/$_4$ cup soft
   margarine
6 oz/175 g/generous ^{3}/$_4$ cup
   superfine sugar
3 eggs
6 oz/175 g/scant 1^1/$_4$ cups
   self-rising white flour
2 tbsp milk
2 oz/55 g semisweet
   chocolate, melted

method

1 Put 21 paper baking cases in a muffin pan, or place 21 double-layer paper cases on a cookie sheet.

2 Put the margarine, sugar, eggs, flour, and milk in a large bowl and, using an electric hand whisk, beat together until just smooth.

3 Divide the batter between 2 bowls. Add the melted chocolate to one bowl and stir together until well mixed. Using a teaspoon, and alternating the chocolate batter with the plain batter, put four half-teaspoons into each paper case.

4 Bake the cupcakes in a preheated oven, 350°F/180°C, for 20 minutes, or until well risen and springy to the touch. Transfer to a wire rack and let cool.

chocolate cupcakes with cream cheese frosting

ingredients

MAKES 18

6 tbsp butter, softened, or soft margarine

3¹/₂ oz/100 g/¹/₂ cup superfine sugar

2 eggs, lightly beaten

2 tbsp milk

2 oz/55 g/¹/₃ cup semisweet chocolate chips

8 oz/225 g/generous 1¹/₂ cups self-rising white flour

1 oz/25 g/generous ¹/₄ cup unsweetened cocoa

frosting

8 oz/225 g white chocolate

5¹/₂ oz/150 g/generous ²/₃ cup lowfat cream cheese

method

1 Put 18 paper baking cases in 2 muffin pans, or place 18 double-layer paper cases on a cookie sheet.

2 Put the butter and sugar in a bowl and beat together until light and fluffy. Gradually add the eggs, beating well after each addition. Add the milk, then fold in the chocolate chips. Sift in the flour and cocoa, then fold into the mixture. Spoon the batter into the paper cases and smooth the tops.

3 Bake the cupcakes in a preheated oven, 400°F/200°C, for 20 minutes, or until well risen and springy to the touch. Transfer to a wire rack and let cool.

4 To make the frosting, break the chocolate into a small heatproof bowl and set the bowl over a pan of gently simmering water until melted. Let cool slightly. Put the cream cheese in a bowl and beat until softened, then beat in the slightly cooled chocolate.

5 Spread a little of the frosting over the top of each cupcake, then let chill in the refrigerator for 1 hour before serving.

This edition published by Parragon in 2008

Parragon
Queen Street House
4 Queen Street
Bath BA1 1HE, UK

Copyright © Parragon Books Ltd 2008

ISBN 978-1-4075-1881-7

Printed in China

Notes for the reader
• This book uses both imperial, metric, and US cup measurements. Follow the same units of measurement throughout; do not mix imperial and metric.
• All spoon measurements are level; teaspoons are assumed to be 5 ml and tablespoons are assumed to be 15 ml.
• Unless otherwise stated, milk is assumed to be full fat, eggs and other individual fruits such as bananas are medium, and pepper is freshly ground black pepper.
• Some recipes contain nuts. If you are allergic to nuts you should avoid them and any products containing nuts. Recipes using raw or very lightly cooked eggs should be avoided by infants, the elderly, pregnant women, convalescents and anyone suffering from an illness.